The House On Savanna Way

AND THE DEMONS WITHIN

A true story of spiritual warfare
by Elizabeth Kristjan

The House On Savanna Way is the true story of
spiritual warfare experienced by a family while
living for nearly three years in a home occupied by
demons. No moment has been exaggerated or
embellished. Names and location have been
changed to protect privacy.

The devil battles for your soul.
In all things turn to God.

Every word of God is pure: he is a shield unto them
that put their trust in him. – Proverbs 30:5

ISBN 978-1-7359451-2-5

DEDICATION

This book is dedicated to my husband John Kristjan, who has my heart and is the better part of me; to my children Mirabella and Giovanni, my precious gifts from God; to the pastors who assisted us, and; most of all to GOD, who loves HIS children and protected us from evil.

Deuteronomy 31:6 – Be strong and courageous.
Do not be afraid or terrified because of them,
for the LORD your God goes with you;
He will never leave you nor forsake you.

Table of Contents

THE BEGINNING

San Elijo Hills, California

John Kristjan and I met on a crisp Sunday morning in 2012, moments after I walked into the church in San Elijo Hills, California, where he was leading worship. He bounced off the stage like Tigger and was in front of me introducing himself before I could blink. I got lost in his deep blue eyes. When he said, *"Hi, I'm John"* I literally thought to myself *Oh no. No no no no no no.* I'm sure I physically backed away from him. The last thing I wanted after a painful divorce was a relationship. I had resigned myself to never date again. I had my two children, my career as a paralegal, and hiking. Majestic mountains and endless trails were out there, calling to be explored. Alone. But we had met. No pushing rewind. If you looked into his dazzling blue eyes, saw his winning smile, movie star dimple, and heard that deep voice, *you would completely understand.* Most importantly though is his beautiful heart. John has that rare quality of balancing strength and kindness. *A rare quality indeed.*

There is attraction and there is love. Attraction drove John to introduce himself the day we met and me to not run. *Genius invention God, this attraction thing.* Love though, that is what grew between us. John possesses the patience of a saint, which is what the man who loved me needed. My ancestors were Scottish, Norwegian, Irish, British, and Native American. I'm stubborn and fiercely independent, with a wicked sense of humor. I have my father's steel blue eyes, my mother's auburn hair, and what my father called "the heart of a warrior". *John was a brave man indeed. And a good man; an incredibly good man.*

John and I dated for three years, slowly getting to know each other and each other's children. He has three and I have two. We moved slowly where they were involved. Early in our relationship John took my then seventeen-year-old son Giovanni ("Gio") to lunch and asked for permission to date me. He was showing respect to my son and to me. *Smart move Kristjan.* My son is Italian. It was crucial to John's survival he ask permission to date me. My daughter Mirabella ("Bella"), then twenty-four had met John at church. *"He's nice"*, she said. Then she proceeded to search every court page and website known to man, the CIA and Interpol, but found no reason why I should not date him. *Thank you sweetie. You are your mother's daughter.*

I met John's children Lucja, Elijah and Agata (ages eleven to four) at church. As time passed they would spend early Sunday mornings at my home while John set up at the church for leading worship. We all got along very well, making pancakes and squeezing orange juice, having

2

lengthy conversations about lizards, art, stickers and multi-colored crayons. I did not know how many different colors of blue Crayola made until Agata showed me. *Had I been living under a rock? Nope, Elijah assured me. That's where the lizards live.*

Slowly the bonds grew.

THE PROPOSAL

Top of the Hyatt, San Diego, California

After three years of dating, John proposed to me one evening at Top of the Hyatt in San Diego, California. This unique roof top bar is forty floors up and offers breathtaking views of San Diego and Mexico. I had introduced him to this location after one of our days spent wandering around San Diego, and he absolutely loved it.

I had a feeling about that night, so I splurged on a sexy new dress. Most of our outings involved hiking boots, fully loaded back-packs, trail maps, hydration tablets, and John's need to know the phone number for the nearest rescue chopper. He had never hiked before we met. The first time I told him, *"You'll be long dead before a chopper can get here, so stop looking"*, he stared at me like I was serious. Our eyes met and the hysterical laughter roared out of me. Definitely more in touch with my Scottish sense of humor while we hike. *Teehehe.* Always the good sport, he laughed too, *kind of.*

Top of the Hyatt has a glamorous edge to it. In my new dress and heels, I felt elegant. A nice change from hiking attire and sunblock.

Shortly after we arrived at this roof top sensation I excused myself to use the restroom, i.e.,

4

stare in the mirror for five minutes checking for any unseemly this, that or the other I may have missed earlier. Oh, and may-as-well use the restroom while I was there. The *I Love Lucy* moment came when I could not unlatch the lock on the bathroom door. *Really?!* The lock was stuck. I don't mean a little bit jammed. I mean STUCK. Not another soul entered the bathroom, nor did I have my cell phone with me. At the thought of calling for help, I envisioned a crowd gathered outside of the bathroom as the firefighters in full gear with hatchet in hand broke through the door. Applause then erupting through the rooftop at my rescue from pending doom. *Mortifying.* I quickly switched gears and wondered what Lucy would do. *She would crawl under the door of course.* DONE! Thank you to every hiking trail that conditioned me to be able to crawl under that door like a ninja. Not a spot on me.

Peril averted and safely seated next to John again, taking in a magnificent sunset view of San Diego, he proposed. Those blue eyes. That kind heart. The patience of a saint. How could I say no? *I never had any intention of saying no. He had me at hello.*

What were four and three became seven when John and I married on the beach in Carlsbad, California on a beautiful day in April 2015.

Now where to live?

THE HOUSE ON SAVANNA WAY

Poway, California

Merging two families together is no small task. John and I had gone to counseling both together and individually to ensure the healthiest of outcomes being blended. We also both lived in homes we were renting. I was in Escondido's Country Club community, a quiet community surrounded by habitat, rolling hills and unique boulder formations. There was a coyote I named Wiley that watched me make breakfast several mornings a week from his perch in the boulders just beyond the fence. He had a direct view into the kitchen, and I had a direct view of him. I had grown used to his visits and welcomed the sight of his inquisitive presence. I once witnessed him face-plant straight into the dirt when chasing a quail. Coyote, zero. Quail, one. *Yes, it was that rural.* John was renting a small house in Poway, in a much busier community.

My son Gio was in college at California State University San Marcos, working on a major in political science and a minor in history. He lived primarily with his father in Carlsbad, which is close by the campus, and the ocean. Gio is very athletic. An avid surfer since he was six; played football through high school; hiking; camping; adventuring. He was an even blend of his father and me, with his father's golden eyes and generous portions of determination from each of us. Dedicated to his friends and family. I felt badly about the prospect of moving an hour away from him. The home I rented in Escondido was close to the campus. He came to my home during breaks between classes and enjoyed homemade meals. My mother's heart loved knowing he was there, having a nice meal made just for him. I knew he wasn't a child anymore. Specifically, because he had told me this... many times. *He needs space. He's a man now.* It was my heart that fought it.

My daughter Bella lived with me, as she worked on paying off her graduate school student loan. I cherished the time with her. Like so many mothers, I dreaded the day she too would not live with me. Not too long ago multiple generations lived together. Arianna, my late mother-in-law told the children and I stories of how she loved growing up in a home filled with her parents, siblings, aunts, uncles, cousins and grandparents. She described so much love in a home full of family. *How did we get away from this?* Bella enjoyed a full life with her friends, and dating. Days would go by without her or I seeing each other. I looked forward to evenings we'd spend watching the latest romantic comedy, or taking a beach walk. I'm amazed at the beautiful, kind, hard working woman she has become.

John's children were still minors. He and his ex-wife shared custody of their children. After leaving John a year before we met, his ex-wife lived with her mother, in a home owned by her mother in Poway. Because his children were younger than mine, we made the decision to live in Poway, until they were older. Bella would live with John and me. She and I would commute to our jobs in Carlsbad, about an hour away in traffic. Thus, began the search for a home to rent.

Cor Meum is a nice community in Poway, situated close to Interstate 15. The first day we began looking for a home to rent, a house on Savanna Way in Cor Meum became available. John contacted the realtor, who was able to meet with us that day. He was a kind younger man, whose wife John knew from the bank he held accounts at. *Such a small world.* We enjoyed chatting with the realtor as we toured the house. Savanna Way is a well-kept, inviting street with freshly manicured lawns and friendly waves hello from people out and about. The name would suggest a grassy plain, but this wasn't the case at all. The streets are lined with Jacaranda trees that yield spectacular purple flowers. Sweetbay magnolia trees and rosebushes grace many yards, which make the neighborhood smell heavenly. The home has a large master bedroom, master bathroom, and extension room off the master bedroom. Lots of space for John and me to lock the door and hide from the children. Newlyweds at any age are *newlyweds*.

There was a wing downstairs, apart from the rest of the house which had a medium sized bedroom and private bathroom. *Perfect for Bella*, I thought. John and I understood she needed her own space. Typically called the "granny flat", this would be a perfect "millennial flat", as more and more of her generation were moving back home to pay off student loan debt. She was being so good about the move. After not finding anything bad on her search of John's entire life, she had grown fond of him, and the children. She approved of the marriage.

The house had four additional rooms upstairs, one for each Gio, Lucja, Elijah and Agata, as well as an oval office area. The oval office was spacious and looked down on the tiled entryway. John could set his home office up here. Lucja was an exceptionally talented artist. The room we picked for her would be perfect for sketching and painting, and gave her a bit of space between her little brother and sister. Elijah was a budding engineer, so he would need enough room for a work bench and his multiple computers. Agata liked unicorns, teddy bears, and making jewelry. She could have the room that faced the street. It got lots of sunshine, which matched her sweet personality.

The house is located close to Interstate 15, which would help with the commute Bella and I would have. There were plenty of parks and trails. This house could nicely accommodate all our needs.

We were sold. At more than four thousand square feet, the house on Savanna Way was perfect. *We signed the lease the day we toured the house.*

FOOTSTEPS

We were not alone

The wedding day and moving day came and went. We began to settle into married, blended life, and our new home on Savanna Way. Summer quickly arrived, and with summer came *extreme heat*. It's not unusual to reach the high nineties in Poway, California in the summer. Living in Southern California is not for those that don't like heat.

While downstairs one afternoon, John and I heard what sounded like someone walking in the master bedroom above us. Strictly speaking, it sounded like someone of a decent weight was walking from where the bed was positioned at the far end of the master bedroom, to the extension room off the master bedroom. *Heavy human steps.* If John had not been standing next to me in the kitchen, I would have thought it was him and dismissed it immediately. *But we were together, in the kitchen downstairs.* This particular day it was John and I alone at home. No children. No pets. We looked at each other and immediately thought, "*intruder*"! It took mere seconds from the time we heard the footsteps to the time we took action. John ran up the stairs at what seemed like the speed of a cheetah, right into the master bedroom. I ran up the

11

stairs right behind him and headed for the thirty aught six rifle. Fear gripped me as I thought my husband was seconds away from engaging in hand to hand combat. *Christ, maybe there was more than one of them!* This increased my speed to the rifle, mindful that I may run smack into a home invader.

I grew up hunting and tracking with my father. I'm no stranger to weapons. One of my favorite pastimes is range day. My mind was racing in high gear. My father trained me for this. I trained my children for this. *Get to your weapon; barricade yourself in a particular space in the house; phone the police; give them your location and let them know you're armed; let the intruder know you're armed; shoot as a last resort. Stay alive.* On this day, barricading was not an option. I trained for this too. *Pursuit.* The would-be victim becomes the hunter. My husband was at risk. I had no choice but to pursue the intruder. *I was praying he or she or they would exit the house immediately.* No one wants to find themselves in this horrible position. Lost in action, loading the weapon, I heard John yell, "There's no one here". *What?!!!* Footsteps are made by a "someone", not a "no one". And those footsteps sounded like a grown adult to me. Rifle in hand, I joined John, not believing the "no one here" declaration. Both our hearts still pounding, we just stared at each other. *"What the hell just happened"* clearly running through both of our minds.

Concerned, we searched every inch of the house, including the attic. *We were indeed alone.* Reaching for an explanation, we reasoned it must be the house settling, methodically, like footsteps. After all, it was hot outside, and this could cause the house to creak. *Maybe this house preferred the sound of footsteps to crackling,* I thought. Now I was just being ridiculous. It was an attempt to push away what there was no explanation for. *We heard footsteps, but we were alone.*

The sound of footsteps continued. When I was at the office John's children would hear this and say to their father, *"I didn't know Elizabeth was home".* He told them it was just the house settling. We told ourselves it was just the house settling. Hearing the footsteps became an almost daily occurrence the entire time we lived in the house.

John and I are both Christian. We believe in God. We believe Jesus lived, died and rose again to deliver us from our sins. We believe there is a spiritual realm. We believe there is spiritual warfare. We understand that if we find ourselves involved in spiritual warfare, we are not to confront the entity. This said, *I don't know of anyone who expects to find themselves in spiritual warfare.* The very thought is bizarre! Because of this, neither one of us shared our thoughts of a presence in the house for quite a while, *when we were finally driven to it.*

INTENSE ARGUING

The honeymoon is over

Every individual who has been married knows there is a honeymoon phase when you are just married. *Birds are chirping beautiful melodies, the sun is shining, rainbows and butterflies are everywhere, and your partner has a halo.* Then the reality phase appears, the phase when you *really* get to know each other. John and I had not lived together before we married, so we knew there would be an adjustment phase. Tragically, what we experienced was *the adjustment phase from hell.*

John and I are best friends. We respect and deeply love each other. A *"Please God take me first"* kind of love. We love each other for the kindness that dwells within; for our outlandish senses humor; for our mutual love of adventure. On any given day one of us could say to the other, *"Do you want to jump off a platform one-hundred-and-fifty feet in the air and sail through the sky tomorrow"?* The response would be *"Sure"*! And we would, if there was zip line reservation space available.

This closeness was shattered when we began to argue just one week into our marriage. These were not minor disagreements resolved peacefully. We were actually *yelling* at each other. We began to

14

behave as if we detested the other person. The trust and love was quickly giving way to a deep dislike for one another. *A darkness fell over our relationship.* The arguments were frequent and fierce. This lasted for months, with brief periods of calm. Our marriage was crumbling before us. The mood in the house turned from joy to hopelessness. We sheltered the children from this, never arguing around them and praying they couldn't sense the tension.

During the week John was at his office and I was at mine an hour away. Thankfully, we had this time to breathe. We were battle weary. We had begun avoiding each other on the weekends too. I would find a reason to be away from him, or he would find a reason to be away from me. We didn't miss each other. We were thankful for the space. Thankful for a break from the war. As a result, a great portion of the time we were around each other was spent *in the house.*

One Saturday several months into our marriage we found ourselves together, *outside of the house.* For reasons unknown, we opened up to each other. We talked for hours about our relationship; the arguments over the tiniest of things; the darkness. Never once during this discussion did we become upset or frustrated with the other. Never once did we disrespect the other person. Our answer to the place we had found our relationship in was *to pray.* Instead of walking out the door we prayed. *We*

15

prayed often and intensely. We lifted each other up to God.

Slowly the darkness began to lift. We again saw the person we loved and wanted to be with. We could *feel* our relationship growing stronger with each passing day. Imagine a category five hurricane with sustained winds over one-hundred and fifty miles per hour slowly giving way to a beautiful, calm sunny day. The storm takes time to subside. *Especially a Cat 5.* The darkness took time to dissolve. Finally, the cold was gone and the warmth had returned. The sailing was now smooth and beautiful.

John and I learned much later each of us had begun working on annulment paperwork and looking for a place to live. We had each absolutely intended to leave the marriage. We also realized much later that the conversation that brought us back together was had *outside of the house*, and that we had taken too long to turn to God.

2 Thessalonians 3:3 – But the Lord is faithful, and HE will strengthen you and protect you from the evil one.

THE VOICE THAT WAS NOT HIS

Revelations of things to come

Several months had passed since John and I stopped arguing. All was blissfully well, except for minor incidents. I was clearly right, he was clearly wrong, and I had to remind him of this. *Not really, but a girl can dream.*

It was in this time something very unsettling happened. John and I had turned in together. It had been a long day and John fell asleep quickly. I was reading while he slept beside me. He's a snorer, which begins slowly, building up to a freight train as the evening goes by. Knowing my window to get into a deep sleep before the train arrived was quickly approaching, I turned off the light and snuggled up to him. I had just gotten comfortable when I heard him giggle. *This was odd.* I had never heard John giggle. He has a *very deep voice.* When he laughs, it's robust. This was definitely a *high-pitched giggle.* He did it again. *Definitely not his voice!* Then he said in that same high-pitched voice with a slight giggle, **"Shhhhh. Be quiet or they'll hear you".** *What the what?!?!* I just about flew across the bed to reach the light on my nightstand. I shook John awake. Violently I'm afraid. Poor guy probably thought I was trying to kill him! I blurted out to him what I had heard. He stared at me, seeing the terror in my eyes, not sure what the hell was happening. It took him mere seconds to wake up completely, which was just enough time for him to think I had completely lost my mind.

John is a warm-hearted man. He loves me fiercely. And apparently, unconditionally. Though I appeared to have gone mad, he lovingly calmed me down. "It was just a dream Beautiful. I was talking in my sleep", he said. "Sounds like I was having a good time. Wish I could remember it." Those deep blue eyes gazing back at me. His arms wrapped protectively around me. Calling me by the pet name he had given me right after we met, *"Beautiful"*. Slowly, I began to relax. *He must have been talking in his sleep*, I reasoned. We laughed about it for a minute. He made me promise I wouldn't assault him in his sleep anymore. I promised. Using a restroom trip as an excuse, I plugged the nightlight in. I heard John give out a little sigh of frustration, but the nightlight stayed on.

ROOM GLOWS RED IN THE NIGHT

Extension room washed in red light

When John and I toured the house one of the aspects that sold us was the size of the master bedroom, and the privacy it would afford us. After all, we were newlyweds. On the left as you enter the master bedroom is a very nice fireplace. There are six large windows in the master bedroom, three of which provide a beautiful view of the green hills that lead to vineyards. After we moved in, we were thrilled to see hot air balloons often. The balloons take off from Del Mar at sunrise and light up the sky with their dazzling colors.

We placed our rosewood bedroom set in the center of the room, which includes a Cal King bed, an extra-large dresser, and two large nightstands. *To my delight, the furniture fit perfectly, w*hich in my mind meant no time would be spent searching for pieces to finish the room. In John's mind this meant no money would be spent on pieces to finish the room. *A win all around.*

The bathroom is on the right as you enter the master bedroom. There is a large walk in closet, which held John and my wardrobes nicely. *Mostly mine.* Wives, you understand this right? Husbands, thank you for understanding this.

Beyond the master bathroom, still within the master bedroom, is an extension room. Basically, it's another bedroom, but it was not closed off. In this room we set up my home office. It was amazingly comfortable and gave me the privacy I needed with office projects, paying bills, stalking people on Facebook, etc. *Don't judge, you know you all do it.*

From our bed, we looked straight into the extension room. Several months after the unsettling occurrence of John talking in his sleep, *"Shhhhh. Be quiet, or they'll hear you"*, and sometime after midnight, *it happened.* I woke from a peaceful sleep, with no immediate explanation. John's slumber was undisturbed. *Sure, sleep like a baby.* A little envious, I repositioned to cuddle with him. It was at this moment I saw it; *the extension room was awash in red!* I froze; transfixed. It wasn't on fire. *It was glowing red!* I couldn't look away. There was no noise. No police light flashing. No ambulance. No firetruck. No sound of teenagers pulling a gag. *Ohhhhh, how I wanted to hear the sound of pranksters.* Silence. Deafening silence. I was horror-struck. A heavy sense of foreboding came over me. I shook John awake. As he woke, the glow vanished. I couldn't believe it. *What the hell was that?!?!* He didn't see it. *Oh my God, he didn't see it!*

We checked the extension room but found nothing out of the ordinary. There was one large window in this room. It was our practice to keep the blinds and black-out curtains closed in the evening for privacy. Even so, we checked outside to see if there was any activity that would have caused the room to glow red, *through the blinds and black-out curtains.* There was nothing. No police car with flashing lights. No fire truck or ambulance. No teenagers pranking the neighborhood. *Nothing.* It was still and quiet.

I knew what I had seen and spent the next few minutes in *sorry, not sorry* mode with poor John. He had been resting peacefully. *But the room was glowing red!* We checked the rest of the house, looking for some sort of explanation. Nothing.

Finally, we went back to bed. No answers. Lots of questions. A heavy, uneasy feeling in the room. There would be no sleep for either of us the rest of this night.

DISAPPEARING JEWELRY

I'm not amused

"John, have you seen my ring"? We had been living in the house about a year and this question had become a regular one. Two of my favorite rings had vanished, along with a beloved bracelet that Bella had given to me. Other pieces of jewelry would disappear, then reappear in places I would not usually put them. Either I was becoming *extremely* forgetful or someone was pranking me. Pondering this, I told myself I was *much too young* for the memory to be going, so it must be a prank. All the suspects were quizzed, but not one person fessed up. This is a group that cracks easily under pressure and has "tells" when they are fibbing. We are all practical jokers, but when the gig is up, the gig is up. The blank stares John and I received made me believe my memory was going after all. *This was not a pleasant thought.*

When John and I were dating he would move something in my home a quarter inch for fun. I can picture him trying to hide hysterical laughter, imagining the moment I realized his deed. It never took too long for me to notice. This is because *I'm a clean freak.* Yes, yes, there is help for that, but I've embraced it. While just messy enough not to be deemed obsessive-compulsive, I am definitely well organized. A place for everything and everything in its place. *Ahhhhh, words that Mary Poppins and I can genuinely appreciate.* Makes John nuts though. He is content to go on a quest through the house when he needs something, knowing he owns the subject of the quest, just not where he has put it. We're polar opposites in this sense. My not putting something in its designated place is extremely out of character.

The first item to disappear was a silver ring with the inscription "For thine is the kingdom, the power and the glory…". [from The Lord's Prayer]

Matthew 6:13 - And lead us not into temptation but deliver us from evil: For thine is the kingdom, and the power, and the glory, forever. Amen

I had worn the ring every day for years; not complete without it. Each evening I took it off before my shower or bath, then put it on in the morning after my shower. Now it was gone. John, the kids and I searched all over the house. We also went to the gym I belong to thinking I may have lost it there. Several times the staff checked lost and found for us, but to no avail.

Months after giving up hope, I found the ring in my jewelry box. It was in a section of the box that I never would have put it. Thanks to my border line OCD, *I knew I had not done this.*

Next to vanish was a silver ring with a raw ruby. I had happened upon this ring in Costco years ago and loved it. I wore it often. It fit well and went with so many of my outfits. Heading out the door one morning I couldn't find it. This was after I had been reconnected with my silver ring bearing the Lord's Prayer. Once again the house was torn apart looking for a ring. Once again, to no avail. I decided it was time to take memory exercise classes. *Where did the ring go?*

Next to go missing was a bracelet Bella had given me when she was in college. It was wooden with beautiful pieces of smooth shell. I wore it often. It vanished about two years into our living in the house. The last place John and I could recall my having it was at Benihana in Carlsbad. We called the restaurant, but they did not have it. We turned the house upside down looking for it. No bracelet.

Interestingly, John and the kids did not experience loss of their items. My memory fully intact in every other way, I became convinced this was a prank perpetrated by one of my stepchildren. *A test perhaps.* Would I lose my temper? Would I forget about it? But none of their "tells" showed and the gig was definitely up! These are great kids. They would never take something that wasn't theirs. So where was the jewelry going? *I was losing my patience with this.* And feeling guilty for suspecting the children.

Jewelry continued to disappear and reappear. *Who was doing this?*

PRESENCE IN THE HOUSE

And there it is

Our first year of marriage flew by. There was the dreadful dark stage, then return of bliss. Our prayers had been answered, and we were stronger for the struggle. Prayer was a part of our daily life, and persistent prayer was answered with peace and tranquility. *There were no butterflies, hummingbirds, or cute woodland creatures dancing around the house with us, but there was joy.* Happiness is a choice and joy comes from God. We are his precious children.

Along with joy came an exceptionally hectic daily schedule. I headed to the law office early every morning, not to be seen until after eight most evenings. I commuted to Carlsbad and would wait out the heavy traffic by going to the gym, taking a beach walk, or meeting my children for dinner. My son lived in Carlsbad and my daughter worked there. It worked out perfectly. I cherish every moment with my children. They are the light of my life.

John was running his insurance business and *"herding crickets"*, his term for parenting Lucja, Elijah and Agata. One of the reasons I fell in love with John was his pure, unconditional love for his children. It was nice to have his children coming and going. During their visits the house was filled with cooking, board games, Uno and refereeing. *Ahhhhh, the sound of children battling over who actually won the game, or who gets to have the last cookie.* I was needed again. This felt good, as my children were grown and pointed this out to me from time to time...and again. I'm sure they hear a helicopter hovering above them each time I call or text. *"Whomp...whomp...whomp...whomp..."* We'll have a real conversation about this when their children are grown. *Yes!*

My daughter Bella lived with us, occupying the downstairs millennial nook and seen from time to time in the kitchen. Post graduate school, she was busy with her career, her friends and paying off a graduate school student loan. She is great with the kids, just like she is with her brother Gio, who is seven years younger than her. I joke with Gio that he has two mothers, me *and* Bella. He is doubly blessed.

When it was just John and I at home, the honeymoon returned. *Marital bliss!* Sleeping in, cuddling by the fireplace, long walks on the beach. Life was good. *What John and I would come to realize is that we were never really alone in the house.* We had all grown used to hearing the footsteps. It was a part of everyday life in the house. The footsteps could be heard while we were downstairs watching television, cooking, cleaning, etc. They could be heard as soon as we entered the house. Some days it sounded like running. Other days walking. But always, we heard the footsteps. The *activity* had increased since we have moved in. Allaying the children's fears that someone was in the house when they heard the footsteps was getting more difficult.

Increasingly, with John lying asleep next to me, I heard the footsteps *right next to my side of the bed.* The room was pitch black from the blackout curtains. The only other person that should be in the room was sound asleep and snoring next to me. *The presence could be felt as easily as the footsteps could be heard.*

I'm a calm person by nature. My parents instilled this in my siblings and I from very young ages. I've pulled a man from a burning car; directed traffic at the scene of a horrific accident on a country road; from the middle of an interstate talked to a woman who was perched precariously on the edge of an overpass sign until the police arrived. *Thankfully, she did not jump.* Remained calm after falling and *severing* my left humerus bone internally. Arteries had been severed. The internal bleeding was massive. I was dying. Laying on the stairs, alone in the house and fading, the words of my mother came to me, "If you panic, you're dead". There would be no panic. I prayed to God to please get me upstairs to my phone. He did.

Emotion only factors into my reasoning after I've exhausted all logical avenues. I had done this since moving into the house; applied logic and stayed calm. I knew, lying there next to my sleeping husband, *there was a presence in the house.* I knew long before him, because *I saw the shape of a person one night by the bedroom door.* This happened on a night when it was just John and I at home. The bedroom door was open, allowing for some light from downstairs, where a lamp by the front door was still on. What has been seen cannot be unseen. *I now lived every day knowing a presence dwelled in the house.*

I did not address the presence when I saw it. It lingered for a few seconds by the bedroom door then vanished. *At the sight of this, terror shot through me. I didn't move in bed. I didn't sit up. I didn't scream. I didn't shake my husband awake. I laid there, looking at it. Then it was gone.*

Frozen in bed for what seemed like hours after the presence vanished, scared to move and breathing only because my body knew to do this, I prayed. I prayed for God's protection over my family. I prayed in the name of Jesus that the presence leave our home. *I prayed to God to protect my family from evil.* I'm sure some people would ask me, "Why do you think it was evil?" *I could feel the evil.*

The next morning, in the light of day I did what every logical person does; I pushed it out of my mind. I said nothing to John. I pressed on with life, as much as any human being could.

It was a long time before I would see the presence again, but every day it let us know it was there, walking through the house, slamming doors, moving things. *Acting oblivious was becoming extraordinarily difficult.*

VOICES IN THE HOUSE

Disembodied

"I hear voices" is not something any sane person wants to admit to another seemingly sane person. *Is John sane?* Mostly. He has three children, who at the time were between the ages of fourteen and seven, two of which are daughters, so allowing him a few insane moments was only right. My children were grown and thriving. I had no reason to be so stressed that I would begin hearing voices. *But I was.*

Well settled in the house I began to hear *conversations.* I thought I was hearing neighbors. I couldn't make out what was being said, but I could hear people talking. *As time went by, the conversations sounded like they were coming from within the house.* Alarming! I quickly banished this thought.

I could never make out *what* was being said. Just whispered conversations. The "what did you say" holler up the stairs or down the stairs, up the hall or down the hall to John or one of the children became a frequent occurrence. I was met with "What? I didn't say anything" all too often. *This was getting frustrating.*

Lying in bed one night, exhausted from the day and ready for a good night's sleep, I realized *the voices were in the room with us, inches from the bed. I could hear a conversation. They were so close!* I could not make out what was being said. The conversation was in whispered tones and went on for a while. Then silence.

These voices I had been hearing were not neighbors, or my family. The voices were not coming from *people*. And there was more than one presence in the house! *And these entities were having conversations!* I could not move. My mind was screaming *"what the hell is going on"?!* My mouth didn't utter a word. We had a problem. *A serious problem.* I suddenly realized it was not John who had said, **"Shhhhh. Be quiet or they'll hear you".** It was them! I was terror stricken!

How do I tell John this? *Do I tell John this?* If someone told me they were hearing voices, I would think they were nuts! *Am I nuts?* A person who has lost grip with reality wouldn't be sane enough to ask that question, *right?*

That night there was no sleep to be had. Besides my heart racing out of my chest, I wondered if the presences would start *talking* again. I wondered if they *talked* all night every night. I wondered what the hell they were talking about. *I felt in my bones we were in serious danger.*

The next day was brutal. I had to get up and go to the office. John wondered why I was so exhausted and all I could say was "didn't sleep well". *Didn't sleep* was more like it. *Traumatized. Terrified.* I had to get in the shower knowing we were not alone. I had to get ready for work and act as if all was normal, knowing we were not alone. I had to keep my thoughts to myself so that whatever had been chatting it up next to the bed would not know I knew. I'm not sure who I was kidding. They could probably smell my fear.

Again, I said nothing to anyone. My sole conversation was with God. I prayed for protection over my family. I carried on. I could not bring myself to tell my husband that I was hearing disembodied voices.

It would be some time before I would utter a word to John about the entities and their conversations. *When I did speak with him I had no choice, the danger had become clear.*

33

SLEEPING ARRANGEMENTS

An unwelcome visitor

What do you get when you put a light sleeper and a heavy snorer together? *Two people that don't sleep.* Two people that must get up in the morning and function in the worlds of insurance and law that haven't slept. This makes for a very unhappy couple and is a potentially dangerous situation for all who encounter us. We should have worn signs that said "Exhausted and Grumpy. Do not approach. Do not piss off". Out of an abundance of concern for each other and mankind, we made the painful decision to sleep separately.

I never thought I would be one of those people who slept apart from their person. BUT IT WAS GREAT! I woke up in the morning refreshed and rested. I had so missed sleep. BEAUTIFUL, WONDERFUL SLEEP! John didn't fare as well. He's up throughout the night due to back problems, plus his snoring wakes *him* up. I should be more sympathetic, but I found myself chuckling at the thought he was waking himself up. *Bad wife.* I don't think he was thrilled with my new exuberance for life. I had to tone my joy down a notch or two, until I left for the office and rejoiced in the birds singing, the sun shining, and not glaring angrily at the person who cut me off in traffic. *"No worries man. You go ahead and go first. Have a great day. Isn't life grand? Hey, by the way I slept last night. Yeah, thank you. I know, right. The world after getting some sleep is beautiful".* If this scene were played out in a sitcom the other driver would be smiling and waving as he passed me in slow motion, an array of colorful flower petals would have been swirling through the air, a rainbow, no a double rainbow would appear, and all the traffic lights would have been green in my favor. Everyone that has slept next to an extreme snorer knows *exactly* what I'm saying.

After the initial catching up of rest, I began to miss having John right next to me; curled up in his protective, strong arms. When he's lightly snoring, he's so cute. When he's full force snoring it's like being present for a thunderous military action. We cuddled as long as we could each night, then he was off to the guest room. He tried every gadget known by his doctors, and those advertised on the radio and internet to curb the snoring. None worked for him. This was now our reality, sleeping separately.

All was well for a few months. I hadn't heard the *conversations* since that night by the bed. I was hopeful prayers had been answered. Though the footsteps remained, I was extremely grateful not to hear any more conversations. There was peace.

Snuggled comfortably in bed, just having turned off the light I felt someone lay down next to me. I thought John had come back into the room. I said, "Hey, I thought you went to bed", and moved to cuddle up to him. No response. "John?" No response. I turned the light on. *No one was there!* I shot out of bed and straight into the guest room, dragging poor exhausted John back to bed with me. I had to tell him I was scared, and why. *It had felt like he had come back to bed,* I explained. *There was that feeling of a grown person laying down next to me,* I told him. Once again, he must have thought I was nuts, but he just said "You're tired. Let's get some sleep". Sweet man. In the morning we reasoned I had actually gone to sleep and had a dream. Sounds logical. I'll agree with that. *I knew it wasn't true.*

A MOTHER'S LOVE

And dancing balls of light

Saturday! *Welcome glorious weekend!* John's children were younger and frequently at the house. We had lots of time to visit. My children, Bella and Gio were grown and busy with their own lives. This Saturday I got together with my children for much cherished quality time. It fills the gap in a mother's heart to see her grown children. Yes, *empty nest syndrome is a real thing.* Though Bella and I lived together, we rarely got to see each other due to both of our hectic schedules. A mother never stops worrying, we just don't let our grown children know this. If we utter any word that even slightly resembles *clinging* in any way, we are then shunned for their chosen amount of time. *A grown child's instinct for independence is strong.*

At the end of this wonderful day, I was ready for a good night's sleep. Shower, check. Heating pad in bed, check. *It was cold outside!* Cuddled with John, check and yay! Time for sleep, definitely. John kissed me goodnight, tucked me in as a show of chivalry, and went to the guest room. I untucked a bit, just enough to breath, and then curled up in his warm just vacated spot. He was an awesome supplier of body heat!

Just after I curled up in John's spot, movement by the bedroom door caught my attention. I stared for a moment and focused. There were three small balls of light *dancing* between the top of the bedroom door and the ceiling. There was no sound. Just three balls moving quickly around each other. This went on for a very short time, less than a minute I would guess, then they were gone. *Had I just seen that? Yes.*

I spent the next hour or so pondering what it could have been that I had just seen. John and I had the lights off while we were cuddling, so my eyes were well adjusted to the dark when he left the room. The balls were clearly *dancing* around each other in swift movements. When they vanished, I got up and checked the curtains. No opening that would have let light in. I laid in bed reviewing every rational explanation I could think of. I was not afraid. There was no heavy feeling of darkness or dread. *I drifted peacefully into sleep.*

In the morning I told John about the dancing balls of light. "Odd" was his response. I couldn't argue that. We had a brief conversation about what could have caused it. An ocular issue was agreed upon and the matter was settled.

A few days later I saw my ophthalmologist. *No issues with my eyes.*

PRUNING ROSES, PICKING FRUIT

And somebody shut the door

The house on Savanna Way is a little over four thousand square feet. It was perfect for our needs, with five children between us and out of state family visiting occasionally. The entrance to the home is impressive, revealing vaulted ceilings, wooden shutters, designer tile, hardwood floor and a beautiful stairway. It has six bedrooms and four and a half bathrooms. It was built in or around 2002, making it about thirteen years old when we moved in. It hadn't been loved on though. We had to give it a deep cleaning, including the garage which had cooking grease, *yes cooking grease,* on the walls and ceilings. We can only imagine what had been going on in the garage.

House and garage scrubbed, we moved in right after our marriage in April of 2015. We added all the designer touches, and in a blink this house was our home. *I call them designer touches. John calls them wasted time and money. Apples. Oranges.* John built shelving in the garage. I added needed touches like window coverings and art to the home. After all of the effort though, John was happy with the feel of the home.

To my and Agata's delight there was a beautiful array of rose bushes in the front yard. We spent hours nursing the roses through the summer. When they bloomed, they were gorgeous! The roses from the yard graced our entrance, our home, our neighbor's homes and our offices. *They smelled fantastic!*

As the seasons changed, we were also thrilled to discover many of the trees in the back yard were fruit trees. We had oranges, miniature bananas, persimmons, crab apples and guava. Sadly, these too had not been loved on, so we got right to work on that. We weren't going to waste God's bounty.

What we were not thrilled to discover is that the air conditioning did not work properly. It wasn't fixed for the first two years we were in the house. We were renting, not sure where we wanted our permanent home to be. The owner periodically sent a repair person out, who dutifully told the owner that the air conditioning was shot and needed to be replaced. This did not happen, which resulted in our having the windows open during the day, and fans on in the evening for two summers. Two summers in 90-plus degrees with no air conditioning. *Not fun.* During this time, doors would close periodically throughout the house. We thought nothing of it because of the flow of air throughout the house. Even when we placed a door stopper in the doors, they would close. Sometimes it was a soft close. Sometimes the door closed with a *slam*. We didn't see this happening. We heard it. If we were upstairs, a downstairs door would close. If we were downstairs, an upstairs door would close. We chalked this up to wind, *extraordinarily strong wind* which we do get in Poway. *Though in the back of my mind, I wondered.*

After being in the house two years, we finally had air conditioning that worked properly. We were now able to close the windows through the heat of spring, summer and fall in Southern California. So, it was a surprise for us when the doors continued to close. If we were upstairs, a downstairs door closed. If we were downstairs, an upstairs door closed. *What the what?!* There must be a sensible explanation, *right?* We checked the hinges on every door in the house. All were working well. We researched houses settling. This could be it we told ourselves, and that was that.

That wasn't that.

EASTER 2016

The arms of an angel

On Sunday, March 27, 2016, I celebrated Easter with my children Bella and Gio after church. Weeks before Easter, I had a bad dream about a car accident. In the dream, a brightly colored Easter egg fell out of a car right after an accident. I remember vividly a mangled car, and the Easter egg rolling slowly out of the wreckage. The dream was very disturbing and stayed with me. When I shared my dream with John, it was more of a warning than a sharing. *I felt as though this accident would happen.* I pleaded with him to drive safely on Easter, and I prayed for protection for my family.

Throughout my life I have received messages from God. Some call this *psychic,* but I know in my soul this is purely God. The messages have always served to protect from pending danger. When called, I have passed these messages on to loved ones and friends. Not all have believed me, but my job as HIS faithful servant is to deliver the message. Sometimes the message is delivered to me through a dream. Sometimes it is more of a feeling, a knowing, or a *memory* flashing through my mind, though the event to cause the memory has not yet happened.

In January 1986, a message was delivered through a car radio. "Wear your seatbelt today" the disc jockey said the second I turned on the car radio. The new seatbelt law was to take affect soon. With a grumble, I snapped my seatbelt into place, not realizing this was divine intervention. Ten minutes into my commute to the office in New Bern, North Carolina I was in a terrible car accident. A genuinely kind woman who was driving the middle-school carpool in her van that morning ran the red light. She was coming out of her community, and later told me she thought the light was green. I was going 55 miles per hour on Route 70 and hit her dead on, as did the van next to me. It was an awful accident. Pieces of the three vehicles strewn across Route 70. The driver that caused the accident and all of the children walked out of the van without a scratch, thankfully. The man driving the other van had a broken leg but was otherwise well. I had minor injuries. *God sent his angels that day, and we were all saved.*

In 1995, when Gio was a toddler, his father, Bella and I were heading out the door to take a beach walk at Torrey Pines State Beach. A feeling stopped me cold. I was not able to walk out the door. When you are a young parent and you have packed up everything like an Olympian, you go where you were headed. If for no other reason than to accomplish the end result of all of the packing. But I couldn't do it. *I couldn't walk out the door.* I looked at my husband and said, "We can't walk Torrey Pines today". He said, "Okay" with no argument. He had known me long enough to roll with it. No questions asked. Just okay. That afternoon a cliff at Torrey Pines State Beach collapsed, killing two men who were on the beach below. They were buried under tons of rocks and dirt. *They were exactly where we were headed, where we walked so often with Bella and Gio. Thank you Heavenly Father for saving my family. Please Lord be with the families of those souls who lost their lives in the cliff slide.* Many times over the years I have prayed for those lost souls and their loved ones. My heart breaks for them.

On Easter Sunday 2016, weeks after the bad dream of the accident, I drove Bella and I to Carlsbad, where we were to meet Gio at the Outlet Mall. The mall was packed with people, as usual. It can be impossible to get a parking spot at the Carlsbad Outlet Mall on the weekend, especially holiday weekends. Seeing an open spot on Car Country Drive, the mall side-street, I took it. It is common for people to stop for a short minute in the median between the west and eastbound traffic on Car Country Drive, like the trucks do to offload new cars onto the car lots. When Gio pulled up, this is what he did. He drove an Audi A4, and would be driving us to the restaurant. Bella got out of my car and into Gio's car. They were both in the Audi waiting for me. I watched for passing traffic, and then got out of the driver's side. Success. No traffic. The speed limit was 25, but people often drove much faster. I then opened the back door, picked up the bag I had Gio's Easter present in, and in one swift movement closed the door, turned and stepped out onto Car Country Drive. *I had not looked for traffic. I had stepped into the path of a speeding car.*

It all happened so quickly but felt like slow motion. My children were in the median, in the Audi. The choice the driver of the oncoming car had was to hit me or to swerve left, *straight into my children.* And the driver of the car was going much faster than 25 mph. *Oh my God!*

In a flash I was against my car. *How was I against my car?!* I had just been in the street. I had just looked at the car bearing down on me, *fast.* But there I was, pinned against my car, instantly away from the danger I had stupidly stepped into. I have no memory of moving from the street to being up against my car. Most importantly, *I could feel the pressure of being held in place.*

I had put my children in such danger when I hadn't looked. I had put the driver of the speeding car in danger. *I feel with every ounce of my being that I was in the arms of an angel; that God intervened and saved all of us that day. HE had warned me to be careful, but I hadn't listened. I hadn't fully understood the message.*

45

This was a significant reminder to me, that whatever was in the house, God was also with us. *HE would never forsake us.*

BELLA'S QUIET TIME AT HOME

Not so quiet

When we moved into the house Bella was managing a retail store in Carlsbad. John and I had set office hours Monday through Friday. Bella's hours at the store fluctuated throughout the week and weekend. This is why it was difficult for us to spend time together, even though we lived in the same house. Bella often found herself alone in the house while John and I were at the office or away for the weekend, which was fine because we all need quiet time. What wasn't fine was the day to day footsteps, doors closing and general feeling of *something isn't right here.*

John and I had gone well over a year without speaking to Bella about what we had experienced in the house. She was an adult, calm and rational, but we thought *why say something that would be upsetting.* We were both praying the *activity* would stop. Less said, the better. And we certainly weren't going to say anything to John's children. If a door closed, *it was the wind.* If footsteps were heard, *it was the house settling.*

In early 2017 Bella decided to take the real estate license exam. She would spend her days off studying. *Bella personifies light.* She has a beautiful soul, always finding the positive, no matter the situation. She is a lovely blend of her European and Native American ancestry, with a slight build, long black hair and stunning dark brown almond shaped eyes. *Always putting others first, her incredible heart shines.*

In looking for a place to study, Bella decided on the kitchen nook table. It was perfect. The kitchen nook is cozy. It was also located directly below the extension room within the master bedroom. It was during this *quiet time* of studying, alone in the house, she began to really listen to the footsteps. She had heard them since we had moved into the house, believing she was hearing the house settling. On her first day of studying though, the activity above her could not be ignored. *She was hearing what definitely sounded like human footsteps, not the creaking of a settling house.* As she sat at the kitchen nook table studying for her exam, the footsteps increased in intensity; there was an urgency in the room above her. It was as if someone was pacing hurriedly, on a mission of sorts. *But she was the only one home.* Enough was enough! She packed up her books and laptop and left the house for a few hours, choosing to study elsewhere. She did not return until John and I were home.

The *activity* in the house was increasing. There was no denying this. That evening, with just the three of us at home, Bella spoke with John and I about it. "I heard a person walking in your bedroom while I was studying". Her face showed alarm, which is unusual for her. This opened up a discussion that would be strictly between the adults in the house.

Prior to this day, John had checked the attic several times thinking it was possible that just prior to our moving into the house, a person or animal could have moved themselves into the attic, and could be roaming around while we were away or in other parts of this large home. But no. The attic was not being inhabited by a human trespasser or an animal.

John, Bella and I had a very frank conversation about the situation. We agreed that none of us would utter a word to the children, and that none of us would engage with whatever it was that was making the footsteps, closing the doors, chatting in the darkness, and cozying up to me in bed.

We prayed for God to protect us from evil; to remove whatever it was that was in the house. We are Christians. We believe *absent from earth, present with God.* We believe there is a spiritual realm. We believe there is a battle between good and evil. We do not believe our deceased loved ones, or any other deceased persons walk the earth. In other words, we do not believe in *ghosts*. We believe in God. We believe there are angels. And we believe there are fallen angels. This is what we believe was in the house, fallen angels, *also known as a demons.*

Revelation 12:7-9 Then war broke out in heaven. Michael and his angels fought against the dragon, and the dragon and his angels fought back. 8 But he was not strong enough, and they lost their place in heaven. 9 The great dragon was hurled down-that ancient serpent called the devil, or Satan, who leads the whole world astray. He was hurled to the earth, and his angels with him.

It is understood in the Christian faith that the devil sends demons to destroy Christians.   To some this may seem far-fetched, especially non-believers in God and the spiritual realm.   I understand.   Even as a Christian, I remember thinking a friend from church was hallucinating when she said she saw demons. I distanced myself from her and never looked back. *I still owe her an apology.*

Now this was *us.* Calm, rational *us.* We were in the middle of spiritual activity. *The worst was yet to come.*

TITAN JOINS OUR FAMILY

The Cane Corso that completed us

When we offered in May of 2017 to foster an acquaintance's dog while he was away for several months, we never imagined this sweet Cane Corso, aka Italian Mastiff, would become our permanent four-legged bestie. But that's just what happened when said acquaintance returned to California and moved in with a woman who had several of her own dogs. After receiving a letter from Titan's owner giving him up, we lovingly made him our own.

Titan's capacity for affection astounded us. If you gave him 100%, he gave you 150%. He truly was our *best friend*. If his big brown eyes couldn't melt your heart, nothing could.

The entire family put in tremendous effort to reassure Titan this was his forever family. He had lost the connection between his former owner and his former owner's ex-wife, whom we had never met. All of the familiar people in his life from puppy to almost five years old were gone from his world. Just like people, animals experience separation anxiety, and Titan was no exception. He didn't like to be away from John or I, *especially John*. He had bonded strongly with John, who we all started calling "Papa" when we were speaking for Titan. I was the one with the treats and the one

51

he behaved for at bath time, but the main person was his "Papa".

The entire family took turns feeding Titan, at which time he was to follow strict commands. A Cane Corso must understand who the alphas are, or they will run your home. He received abundant kisses and hugs from the girls and wrestling from the guys. He took beach walks and had dinner at Norte and other outdoor restaurants in Carlsbad with Gio, Bella and me. He went hiking with John and I, and walks by the lake with John and I, and Lucja, Elijah and Agata. *He was home, with his people.*

In return for the boiled chicken, carrots, pumpkin and various other yummy dinner items; very large rawhide bones to gnaw on; treats; blankets, etc., he showered us with love, and his form of protection. If a bird flew into the backyard, he was on it. If someone dares walk even close to any part of the yard, he was on it. Weighing in at 125 pounds of muscle and teeth, his bark was most definitely an indicator of his potential bite. Cane Corso loosely translates from Italian into English as *Guardian Dog*. Though with the family it was cuddles and love. *And gas.* The Cane Corso is often referred to as the "Roman Dog of War". History tells us they accompanied Roman soldiers into battle. I'm convinced that the Roman soldiers merely lined their K9 partners up and ordered them to gas the enemy. *Yes, it's that bad.*

Titan was comfortable in most of the house. The master bedroom was different. I've heard in the past animals can sense what cannot be seen, but I had never given it much thought. Often Titan hesitated to move forward into the master bedroom, stopping short at the door and staring at John or I. What seconds before was a bouncy, energetic dog turned into an extremely reluctant dog. The worst of it occurred one evening when I ran a bath. Titan did not want to leave me alone in the bathroom. He was anxious, whining and moving in circles near the tub. Several times he ran to get John, who reassured him it was okay. "Mama is just taking a bath", John said to him, then led him out of the room, only to have Titan run back into the bathroom, ultimately pressing himself as much as he possibly could against the bathtub until I emerged from the water, giving up and listening to him. *"I guess it's not bath night big guy",* I said giving him a hug. He was so new to us, I thought he was afraid of the water. Looking back, John and I strongly believe he sensed a presence was there. Brave dog. He could have hid under the kitchen table downstairs, but he stayed with me. *Titan has our hearts forever.*

CREEPY CRAWLERS

Invasion of the Earwigs

Southern California is no stranger to earwigs, those tiny multi-legged insects with pincers. In spring of 2017, several earwigs appeared on the master bathroom floor in the house. I shrieked appropriately, in hopes my wonderful husband would kill them. He did. *My hero.* After he disposed of the corpses, I told him they gave me the creeps. He teased me about it, *"You hike mountains and forests, sleeping under the stars in mountain lion and bear country, and you're creeped out by tiny bugs",* laughter bursting out of him. *"Bugs belong outside"* I told him, not being able to keep from laughing myself. After all, he was right. His fearsome hiker wife was a sissy girl when it came to bugs in the house.

That evening we pulled down the comforter and discovered an earwig between the sheets. *Ewwwwwww!!* John the assassin took care of this one too. *Thank you honey.* I had never seen one in a bed. We do not eat in bed, so there would be no food to attract them. My border-line OCD regarding neatness ensured sheets were washed at least once per week. *Now I was totally freaked out.* I removed and washed the sheets and pulled the mattress off looking for more. None found, thankfully. I double-checked under the bed, vacuumed the entire room and dusted. Half-way through my exterminating frenzy, John went to bed in the guest room. Finally satisfied with the condition of the room, I went to bed, snuggled up in fresh sheets.

A moment after I turned off the light, I felt a sting on my leg. *Ouch!!* I flew out of bed and pulled back the sheets. There, in the middle of the bed was an earwig! *How the hell?!* I had cleaned everything and put fresh sheets on the bed. Exhausted, bewildered and creeped out, I slept on the couch that night.

When I got home from the office the next evening, John and I talked about the *earwig event* of the night before. It must have just been one of those freak things we agreed. Several hours later, both of us ready for a good night's sleep, we pulled down the comforter and were shocked to see over a dozen earwigs in the bed! *They were crawling all over the sheets! They were everywhere! It was an earwig invasion!* I distanced myself from the bed in a split second! Brave John tore the fitted and flat sheets off the bed and ran out to the back yard with them. Several ended up on him. *Definitely my hero!* He repeated this with the comforter. While John was busy with extermination, I began the cleaning regimen of the night before in earnest, not seeing another earwig anywhere. I opted to sleep on the couch again, *just in case.*

This continued for several weeks. *Pull down the sheets, find several earwigs.* With each passing day I was becoming less alarmed to find the pesky buggers in the bed. *I became an earwig killing machine, desensitized.* I expected to see an earwig when I pulled down the covers. So, several weeks later, when there wasn't one, I was surprised. *Very pleasantly surprised.*

That was the end of the invasion. John and I chalked it up to Southern California living. What was especially odd was that this only happened in the master bedroom. There were no earwigs found in any of the other five beds in the house. *Actually, there were none seen anywhere else in the house.*

About a year after moving out of the house on Savanna way we realized the earwigs were no longer found in our bed when I quit having a negative reaction. *The activity stopped when I was desensitized.*

DANGEROUS INTENT

The entities get physical

At a certain age, a person cannot help but make at least one bathroom trip in the night. I'm no exception. At least once a night I drag myself to the biffy, missing my youth with every step, a barely conscience, blurry-eyed version of myself. Maybe if I didn't down so much iced tea during the day, or sip a hot chocolate after eight o'clock, I could get some rest. *Nope.* I want the hot chocolate with extra whipped cream and mocha drizzle. Yes please!

Groggily trudging to the bathroom by the glow of the nightlight one evening, I almost ran straight into the edge of the shower door. Startled, *"What the bleep!"* came loudly out of my mouth. Only, I didn't say "bleep". The shower door was one-half inch thick glass. It was beautiful and *solid.* The door wasn't open a little. It was open almost 90 degrees, which placed it directly in the path of the bathroom door. *Literally right in front of me when I turned the corner.* It was by the grace of God I didn't run straight into it. With the right impact, I could have been hurt. I thought I must have left the door open after my shower, and was grateful I had recently begun lighting up the room with a nightlight. Back to bed, the incident was soon out of my mind.

The next evening it happened again. Luckily, I had approached with more caution. After several nights of this, I assumed the door's catch was off and mentioned it to John. He examined the door. It was fine. It had a magnetic catch that was working perfectly.

Sometime between my going to bed and the after-midnight bathroom trip, *the door was opened.* I never heard a sound.

One afternoon while John was examining the shower door again, I commented to him this was only happening at night. After that conversation, the door was opened during the day as well. *What the hell?!* This happened whether it was just John and I at home, just me at home, or a full house. No one in the family would do this. *It was dangerous.*

Eventually the shower door was replaced. The new catch was a spring-loaded hinge. Water had been leaking into the wall and down through the kitchen ceiling, so the shower was remodeled. However, the heavy shower door continued to be consistently opened during the day and night for the duration of our stay in the home.

Because of John's snoring, he slept in the guest bedroom. This never happened to him. The *activity* seemed to largely be in the master bedroom, where I was. *This activity could have harmful consequences.*

MEDICINE CABINET DOOR
SLAMS SHUT

Unsolicited "help"

The life of a paralegal is a busy one. It's up early and out the door to the office, the court or county recorder. Grab the briefcase and lunch. Kiss the husband, pet the dog, and just like that you're off and running for the day. This means rushing the morning beauty routine if one wakes up a bit late, which happened more times than I care to admit.

On one of these rushed mornings I was moving quickly at the bathroom sink, swift motions that would make an Olympic bobsledder envious. Unruly hair softened and temporarily obeying. Check. Face lotion with SPF, foundation, eye shadow, mascara, check, check, check and check. Time for lipstick, the final touch. I raised my right arm at lightning speed, on a collision course with the partially open medicine cabinet door. *The very thick, sharp edged, mirrored medicine cabinet door.* As my arm was in motion, the medicine cabinet door closed with a slam, breaking the glass mirror. An immediate, intentional closing. *Only not by me.*

After the initial scream, I stood motionless at the sink in stunned silence. Frozen. Struggling to comprehend what had just happened. Like the other doors through the house, this one had just slammed shut. The difference? *It happened right in front of me.*

When John raced into the master bathroom he found me standing at the sink shaking. He glanced between me and the medicine cabinet several times. He had no explanation. Nor did I.

We agreed again that something wasn't right about this house. *Not right at all. Terrifying actually.*

I'M NOT ALONE IN THIS BED

The uninvited visits continue

From the time we moved into the house, we heard footsteps in the master bedroom. At first, we reasoned it away. As time went by we realized *something* was in the house. Actually, several *somethings*. This is true too for the sensation of someone lying down next to me in bed. Initially, I dismissed it as not being fully awake, or simply imagination. Maybe there was a small earthquake, and that is why the bed moved. I don't drink. I don't take drugs. It must just be my imagination. *Right?* Wrong.

After the medicine cabinet door closed the sensation that someone was lying on the bed increased greatly. It was obvious; no way to ignore it or reason it away. To attempt to would be likened to ignoring when John laid down next to me, acting like he wasn't really there. Blankets were moved. The mattress shape changed. Cold air wafted my face, sending a chill through my entire being. *It was terrifying.* Often, I went to get John, dragging the poor guy into the room, fear covering all of me. We'd lay there half the night, not able to get back to sleep. Waiting. Expecting it would happen again. It didn't. Not while John was there. Other times I lay frozen, or went downstairs to read, turning every light on along the way. Sleeping wouldn't happen.

Through all of this we prayed. We never directly addressed whatever was in our home. I began laying the Bible next to me in bed, where "it" was laying. I put a wooden cross from Israel on the pillow next to me. I had no idea if this would make the entity stop laying down next to me, but this made me feel better.

I believe in God the Father, the Son and the Holy Spirit with all my heart and soul. I believe HE dwells in me. I believe I am HIS child. I began to speak with God out loud as I lay down to sleep each night. I prayed for protection and thanked HIM for being my Father. I asked for guidance and wisdom. I prayed for protection for my family from evil. I prayed for strength. I prayed for peaceful rest. *And that is what I received.* After I prayed out loud, the entity did not lie next to me. Realizing this, I prayed out loud every night until we moved from the house. *We needed God, HIS love, mercy and protection.*

A DEMON SHOWS ITSELF

Movie night severely interrupted

It had been a particularly busy week. John and I were looking forward to a peaceful Saturday night. It was just the two of us this weekend. After housework all day, which included endless laundry, vacuuming, mopping, etc., we settled in around 8:00 p.m. to watch a movie. Hot chocolate with homemade whipping cream and a dash of nutmeg in hand, we turned on *Pirates of the Caribbean: Dead Men Tell No Tales.* We've enjoyed this series and had been looking forward to finally seeing the fifth edition. It was early 2018.

In the house on Savanna Way, as you come down the stairs, you enter into the family room, which is directly under the master bedroom. This is where John and I were watching the movie. He was on the couch, centered in front of the flat screen television which hung on the wall. I was to his right, in one of our big blue chairs. My aging back loved this chair!

As you enter the family room there is a switch on the wall to the left. This controls the ceiling fan. The fan has three settings; low, medium and high. *The wall switch was off.* When you turn on the wall switch, the fan is designed to turn on the light first, then you have to manually switch the fan from low, to medium, then to high. We rarely used the ceiling fan in the family room, especially this night, while the weather was still cool.

Focused on the movie, which had been on about fifteen minutes, I saw movement to our left, at the entry to the family room. *The silhouette of a man was standing right next to the light switch!* At what seemed like the same second I screamed, "John!", the fan began whipping at the maximum speed above us. At that moment the fan light didn't turn on. The fan was instantly at full speed! This is the OPPOSITE of how the fan is designed to function. I screamed, "there's a man at the light switch!" Then it was gone. I had seen it! There it was! *In a split second it vanished.*

We don't know if turning the fan on full force was a distraction by the entity because it had been seen, or if this was what it was going to do all along. The entity at the light switch was the form of a man, but not how we appear. It was the *form* of a man. I don't know if I'll ever be able to properly describe this. Clearly human form, seemingly male build, but not fully there. Frustrating to explain.

John ran to turn the fan off, looking just as shocked and bewildered as I had been since moving into the house. We spent the next few minutes trying to understand this. Finally, we looked at each other and said, "let's go upstairs". Feeling like we were no longer supposed to be in the family room, or the house altogether.

After we had calmed down a bit, we texted several of our neighbors whose homes were in close proximity to us, and asked what kind of fan they had, thinking one of their remotes may have triggered our fan. Nope. Of course, the wall switch, aka *the power for the fan was off*, so I'm not sure why we bothered to contact the neighbors. And of course, we didn't tell them what I had seen, just that the fan had turned on. Impossible, without the power on. And certainly not to full speed in a split second, bypassing all other functions. *We tried to duplicate this, but could not.*

Message sent. Message received. *John was present this time.* Though he had not seen the entity, he saw the act.

The day after the "fan incident", which is what we've chosen to call it, John contacted an old friend and pastor, Brad. After explaining in detail what we had been going through since moving into the house, Pastor Brad agreed there were demonic entities in the house. He shared with us a prayer that had been successfully used in the same sort of situation we unfortunately found ourselves in.

We were instructed to pray in each room of the house and anoint each door frame with anointing oil, which we did. Anointing oil is mentioned in the Bible many times and represents the presence and

66

power of the Holy Spirit. After doing this, we felt an immediate peace.

The peace would not last. *The entities were not going anywhere.*

SCREEN DOOR RIPPED FROM ITS TRACK

A plea for help to our local pastor

Each evening we prayed. Each evening the shower door was left open, the footsteps persisted, and muffled conversations were heard throughout the house. The entities were intentional in making themselves known.

One afternoon in March, John and I met at the house for lunch, both having offices close by since I left the Carlsbad office for one near home. We let Titan out for some sun in the backyard and were eating our lunch at the kitchen island. We were both looking in the direction of the screen door, expecting Titan to appear. Instead, there was a thunderous *"BAM"* against the screen door. It was ripped from its track, landing on the patio outside. *What the hell!?!?* We both saw the blow to the screen door happen. We just didn't see *what* did it. After a few seconds we walked over to the screen, then checked on Titan in the backyard. He's a Cane Corso. This is no weak, timid dog, yet he was frozen in place, trembling, looking in the direction of the screen door. *Now we were pissed!!* I held myself back from what I wanted to do, *curse the things out and send them back to hell!* John felt the same. As Christians, we knew not to address the entities directly. We were extremely frustrated. And we were angry. Extremely angry. *We assume that's what they wanted, anger.*

John phoned our local pastor that afternoon and scheduled an appointment to meet. We needed his guidance and help from our brothers and sisters in Christ.

The day of our meeting, our pastor became very ill. A member of the church staff phoned John and cancelled the appointment. Another month went by before we would meet. Another month of amped up activity by the entities. We learned later from our pastor that the illness fell over him suddenly and left him just as he got home from the church office. Odd. We felt badly, discussing the possibility that this happened to him because we had an appointment to discuss the entities in our home. We have no proof, *just a feeling.*

During our meeting we laid out in detail what had been happening in the home since we had moved in. We told him of our prayers and the advice from Pastor Brad. Our Pastor was at a loss. He was well intended but didn't know what to do. He told us this was not his area of expertise, confusion and concern spread across his face. *He probably thought we had lost our minds.*

Very much needing help, we discussed with our Pastor the possibility of willing members of our church praying at the four corners of the house. We are private people, so this was a huge expression of our need. He said he would think about this. He prayed with us, and then the meeting was over. We have high respect for this man. He is exceptional at leading his congregation to Worship. He is a humble and kind man. He was right. This was out of the expertise of many. We didn't blame him for distancing himself from the situation. *We continued to pray.*

GOD HAS SPOKEN

An answer to prayers

From the time we moved into the house on Savanna Way we heard footsteps. In the almost three years that had passed, the entities had slowly revealed themselves to us. They taunted us. They hid our things, opened doors, closed doors, slammed doors, laid in bed next to me, appeared physically twice, terrified the dog, attempted to harm me with the shower door, damaged the screen door, and threatened our emotional well-being. *Things amped up when we started praying over the house.* We had prayed to God for removal of the entities from our home. They were still there. We had prayed for protection. No member of our family was ever harmed. *We believe fully this is due to God's protection. The entities clearly had the ability to harm us.*

In late April 2018, while driving up CA-18 to hike Big Bear, John's phone rang. It was the owner of the home. He informed us that he would not be renewing our lease. He told John he needed the home for members of his family. When John hung up and told me, I began to cry. Sob actually. I still cannot explain that reaction. We needed to get away from this house and had been looking ourselves for another home, but to no avail. It seemed we were stuck. Now we *had* to move. This was such a relief. *God had spoken.* The entities wouldn't leave, so God was removing us from the situation.

After the screen incident, we had stopped discussing the entities while we were in the house, believing discussing how they were affecting us would give them power. Now we would be discussing a move. We would be packing, happily. We braced ourselves for reaction from the entities, praying there would be none. *There was.*

SEARCH FOR A HOME

And increased unrest in the house

When John and I returned from hiking, we busily began the preparations for a move. Being so newly married, and blended, we weren't ready to purchase a home. We weren't sure where we'd like to live when John's children were older, so renting was still a fit. We activated our Zillow, Trulia and Redfin accounts, and the search was on. The results... *nothing*. The owner of the house on Savanna Way had given us seven weeks' notice. Though we were having difficulty finding a home to rent, we began packing, not knowing where God would take us. Frustrated with the lack of what was out there, we kept our faith. We walked through what seemed like endless dilapidated, unkempt homes. *The health department needed to be told about a few of these "homes".* I felt myself giving in to the frustration, a darkness coming over me. *John and I were both exhausted.* Between our busy work schedules, packing and the search for a home, there was little time to rest. The pressure was on. And we were both feeling the stress.

With each box that was packed, the tension in the house grew. John and I continued to pray, and with each prayer the entities ramped up activity. More movement, more shower door openings, more chatter next to the bed, more door slamming, items being knocked off the counter in the master bathroom in the middle of the night, kitchen cabinet doors found wide open throughout the day and night, what sounded like running in the master bedroom, *constantly*. We learned there was no use in asking ourselves *"why"*. It's like asking why a person would harm another person without provocation; evil. *Pure evil.*

Towards the end of our stay in the house, something extremely odd happened, *the remaining missing items began to reappear.* While packing, I began to find treasured jewelry that had vanished. The beloved bracelet that Bella had given to me years before, that had gone missing about a year after moving into the house, was found under my sun hat in the master bedroom closet. I had worn that sun hat multiple times since the bracelet had gone missing.

The silver raw ruby ring that I use to wear almost daily and that had vanished soon after moving into the house was found in a crystal dish in my home office, amongst the potpourri. I had cleaned that dish many times since the ring had gone missing. *It was not there before.* After the initial confusion, I reasoned how the ring got there. I'm a neat freak, who puts things where they belong as soon as I take them off. I didn't do this; they did. *But why? Why take these items? Why return them now?*

THE NEW HOUSE

Serenade of the doves

The weeks had pressed on with no viable option from the houses we had toured. The houses were either filthy, too small, or no large dogs were allowed. John and I both understood, having owned our own homes in the past, and having been landlords ourselves. Of course owners desire to protect their property. We are neat, clean people who leave a home in better shape than we find it, and Titan is a sweet dog. He's not destructive in any way and rarely barks. But once we told homeowners our dog is a Cane Corso and they looked it up, fear and panic crossed their faces. *"Light the torches. Kill the beast!"* could clearly be seen in their eyes. *Ugh. Sigh.* The Cane Corso makes an excellent family pet. They are great with children, and are not destructive. They do look fearsome and have to be trained well, knowing who the alpha is, but they do possess wonderful dispositions. There are many small dogs that are the worst offenders. "Don't judge a book by its cover" applies here. *Don't get mad. I love all dogs.* Well, all except the Jack Russel Terrier who attacked my leg years ago while on a walk through my neighborhood. This was a neighbor's dog. He was a very nice person, however his dog was a terror! Yet it was exactly the type of breed most landlords were okay with. *Seriously?!*

We had been searching for five weeks. To say we were stressed would be a gross understatement. We were all packed and nowhere to go. I began to wonder if the entities had anything to do with this. Ridiculous. *Or was it?* We continued to pray, our faith in God never wavering. *Our stress with the activity in the home mounting.*

On June 15, 2018, John saw a listing for a house. It was smaller than the house on Savanna Way, and in a rural town to the north of us, but it looked good in the photos and the commute to work was doable. We scheduled a tour immediately and were there that afternoon. The house was situated at the end of a cul-de-sac and had beautiful landscaping, a desert-scape that reminded us of the Baja Gardens at the San Diego Zoo Safari Park, (forever the *Wild Animal Park* to locals, and one of our favorite places).

The real estate agent who met us was very pleasant. She showed us through the home and gave us a bit of history. It had been vacant for just over a year, while being renovated by the new owner. He had purchased the home as an investment and was ready for the right tenant. Actually, he was way past due for the right tenant and beginning to wonder if it would ever rent. *Odd. The home was gorgeous and should have been rented immediately after being listed.* The kitchen was beautiful with brand new appliances, which included double ovens. The countertop was granite and the backsplash was done perfectly. There was crown molding throughout the home and the carpeting was new. To add to this, there was a deck off the master bedroom that provided sprawling views of the hills and amazing sunsets. The home backed up to habitat. The backyard also had the desert-scape, beautifully done. *This place was a dream!*

After doing a bit of research on-line about the house and the neighborhood, and not finding anything negative, we submitted our application. We heard back the next morning. The owner asked how soon we could move in. *We had found our new home. Praise God!*

The next two weeks were a blur of activity; reserving a moving truck, finishing the packing, changing our address with the USPS, doctors, dentists, loved ones, and in every profile we've ever created online. *Wheeeeee!* But we did it with joy. *We were leaving the house on Savanna Way and the demons within.*

We shared the good news with our children. Bella had moved to San Elijo Hills, California, to be closer to work. Gio was working on his bachelor's degree and living in Carlsbad. They both, along with Bella's boyfriend Christoph helped us on moving day. Even though the occasion was a move, it was nice to spend time with them. *A mother's heart will take every moment with her children she can get.*

The activity in the house went still a few days prior to the move. This was odd. *I didn't trust this.* It was too quiet. A sudden panic gripped me. *What if they went with us?! Oh my God! No!!!* We prayed heavily against this.

On June 30, 2018, we moved to the new house. Making trips back and forth the next few days to get the last few belongings, sweep the garage, clean the carpet, etc. On July 3rd we handed over the keys. *Our independence day.*

On July 5th John left with his children for a cross-country trip, which would include stays at several national parks. I would miss them, but this house felt different. It gelt good. It was peaceful. *There was a light.* I slept through the night, for the first time in a very, very long time.

On July 6th, my first morning waking up alone in the house, I woke to a strange sound. There was a noise. *A living noise.* Titan had been sleeping on his blanket on the floor next to my bed. He rose quickly and searched for the source with me, fur raised, low growl humming from his broad chest. I was trembling at the thought the entities had moved with us. *No, no, no, no, no, no.*

To my relief and joy, the noise was coming from a flock of doves that were perched on our roof. *Doves. We had doves on our roof.* *Hallelujah!* While this might bother many, I was thrilled! I went back to sleep to the cooing of the doves, knowing God had placed us in a safe home filled with HIS light

Thank you, Father.

THE HOUSE ON SAVANNA WAY

Post move

John and I have stayed in touch with our neighbors from Savanna Way, however we never shared with them the events that we experienced. With regards to the entities, we wanted to close the door behind us, hand over the keys and forget all that had happened there.

Ultimately, I was called to tell the story. A nudge. A tug. *A calling to write my testimony, for the Glory of God.* While this happened to our family, I experienced most of the activity. John and I prayed and had many conversations before proceeding with the testimony. *This has been difficult.* We've prayed over the writing and relived many moments we would much rather forget.

Our former neighbors have told us of the screaming they hear coming from the house. "The new neighbors are always fighting", one neighbor told us. "Strange music comes from that house", another neighbor told us. Again, we've never shared our experience with our neighbors. As I was finishing this book one of our former neighbors phoned. She asked that I be a reference for a job that she had applied for. Of course I would; she was a wonderful person. We chatted for a while about her potential new job, children and when to get together for dinner. Then, without prompting, she said, "There's something odd about your old house. The couple who moved in were always fighting, screaming at each other at all hours. They divorced and she took the children. He's now on his third girlfriend, and he's always screaming at them. It's dark over there except for red lights inside, and strange music. His dogs are always digging to get into my yard. They seem afraid".

It seems the entities have been busy. Brothers and sisters in Christ, please pray for the occupants of The House on Savanna Way. We lift them up to the Lord, we ask protection and that they would know you Lord. Amen.

BATTLE FOR SOULS

Spiritual warfare is real

When I felt the calling to write my testimony, *I didn't want to.* I fought it. The last thing I wanted to do, the last thing John wanted to do was relive the spiritual warfare we had left behind. But the calling grew stronger as time passed. After much prayer, *this is my testimony.* Spiritual warfare is real. It's ugly and terrifying. It's not exciting or intriguing. NEVER GO LOOKING FOR THIS. It's an awful thing to experience, and extremely dangerous. *It's a battle for your very soul. Be vigilant!* God is more powerful than darkness. God protects HIS children. *God protected us and delivered us from the evil that dwells in the house on Savanna Way.*

Ephesians 6: 10 Finally, be strong in the Lord and in his mighty power. 11 Put on the full armor of God, so that you can take your stand against the devil's schemes. 12 For our struggle is not against flesh and blood, but against the rulers, against the authorities, against the powers of this dark world and against the spiritual forces of evil in the heavenly realms. 13 Therefore put on the full armor of God, so that when the day of evil comes, you may be able to stand your ground, and after you have

*done everything, to stand. 14 Stand firm then, with
the belt of truth buckled around your waist, with the
breastplate of righteousness in place, 15 and with
your feet fitted with the readiness that comes from
the gospel of peace. 16 **In addition to all this, take
up the shield of faith, with which you can
extinguish all the flaming arrows of the evil one.**
17 Take the helmet of salvation and the sword of the
Spirit, which is the word of God.*

If you're having a similar experience, please
pray. Consult the Bible. Contact your pastor.
*Never engage the entity. Don't invite darkness into
your life. Fight against it!* If you've not yet given
yourself to Jesus Christ, *please do.* Only through
HIS power can spiritual warfare be overcome.
Speak to him, as you would a loved one. Pour your
heart out to him.

Made in the USA
Middletown, DE
15 May 2022

65780712R00057